PRAISE FOR *OUTSIDE VOICES, PLEASE*

outside voices, please moves the mundane and intimate violence of English-as-axis-language outside, where it plays out as gash, ripple, unforgivingly abrupt verses, fragments, and something loud enough to disrupt the propriety of colonialism. Hsiung writes, "Give me an English map / and I will show you an English love, an English rape(d) word." Her work brings what has been discarded as noise into verse, turning its back on the imperative to render entire worlds meaningless through erasure. —RAQUEL SALAS RIVERA

. . . tests murmur slur, blurs outburst tantrum codes inside translation . . . cracking performativity. . . refugee slippage of CAST OF MANY . . . this book is a bravery . . . mess and moss "becoming the weapon" . . . "you now have two minutes to run outside" pick it up, be brave, say yes . . . —GABRIELLE CIVIL

T0303145

Hsiung's *outside voices, please* is densely synaptic, a rewarding cascade within the confines imposed by our well-realized but half-understood systems of meaning, living, and language-making. The lens of this collection zooms in and out intuitively, prompting the reader to incorporate the cellular, molecular, and viral along with the vastness of the conceptual and cosmological. Hsiung shows us that very connection has an impact, and every encounter changes us. Something gets transformed, something gets left behind, something remains itself, something is a testament to the coercion of change, something is the singing that persists under power differentials. Something, something, something—it's all in the voices and stories told from the outsiders who intelligently, devastatingly acknowledge their histories and futures in this collection. Smells, textures, memories, visions, electrical connections, and the lived outcomes of political power-play, in all their forms, are included in this worldview. There is also the pleasure that Hsiung's poetry provides, the drumbeat wordplay that flexes your face and heart as you read over the sedulous and unexpected associations that both reflect and meaningfully distort our saturated world stage. To read the world through *outside voices, please* is to feel challenged and also to feel seen. Are you ready to enter? —GINGER KO

To enter into the text of *outside voices, please* is to plunge into a voice made of all voices, a whirring concert of murmurings, glossolalia, commands, scat and static—the sounds the mind picks up from sheer being. This Voice then articulates the ironies, and the sadism of being stuck in a society that doesn't want freedoms for you, that sets you against others in a market system run on basic desires, that sees its idea of you instead of actual you. The reader's pleasure is in gleaning a wry defiance... all of this through the chords by which the speaker's mind is struck. Here I learned what the intersection of race, sex, diaspora, and listening sounds like: a phenomenal—and dear—ocean. —CYNTHIA ARRIEU-KING

outside voices, please

outside voices, please
FIRST EDITION

DESIGN ≈ SEVY PEREZ
Adobe Caslon Pro & Europa

This book is published by the

Cleveland State University Poetry Center
csupoetrycenter.com
2121 Euclid Avenue, Cleveland, Ohio 44115-2214

and is distributed by

SPD / Small Press Distribution, Inc.
spdbooks.org
1341 Seventh Street Berkeley, California 94710-1409

A CATALOG RECORD FOR THIS TITLE IS
AVAILABLE FROM THE LIBRARY OF CONGRESS

outside

voices,

please

valerie

hsiung

TEST

... so the volt was all wrong. Circle clo-
sing/closed the bottle, we were spec-
tacles. I said fascinated I was, by germ
theory, like horror. I said I was given sten-
cil once to trace postulate, but I fell ba-ck-
wards, to the eraser's ash. I sleep now in
a storage cubicle where It is honored to
wear a winter hat. I submit to It wi-th-
in ideal temperatures, form gaming
instructionals and forearm calluses in-
stead of cities...

... girl woke up deaf today... girl woke up
hugging trike... girl woke up deaf and mot-
her at the console... girl woke up with h-
er wick in a net, witness her collection of mu-
gs, tally It down a notch, witness her mu-
g-shot prior to crime, It's a tree, of the n-
otched, as of threes in a bra, It's a tree, and It
won't be consoled until you denote back t-

o us, toothy, pithy one, girl girl, we're swig-
ging from the mug and the trees are all pa-
cking to one another and I am dread toni-
ght of who we truly are, Alexander Gra-
ham Bell, founder of AT&T...

... a visit to the herbalist for otorhinolar-
yn-go-logical issues. Were you a fighter?
Yes. I was a fighter. The herbalist exam-
ines her tongue with a set of herb tongs.
But there's a flu going around, isn't th-
ere? Yes. There's a flu going around. Th-
is is not the flu though. The herbalist ta-
kes the tongs now to the cage. With max-
imal effort. I caught the news this morning.
And then I went to the end and caught
my horoscope. You don't chew proper-
ly? No. I don't chew properly. I gesticul-
ate rennet, pronounce one's the ditch w-
ith a chained-up microphone, announce th-
e guillotine at the epiglottis...

… which was plight. It said you were a d-
read man. but It knew no dread. which was I-
ice. It said It knew no man who worship-
p-ed dread could be turned. which was cong-
enital. proclivital. and blame the women
guards at the death camps more than we've bl-
amed the men. debacle opens to dead chil-
dren in their school chairs with their half-
raised arms frozen-limp. I don't know wh-
en this was all set to go to hell for us but
for now it seems important to declare th-
is is real, to each other…

… and if a man is turned into smear…
and, if, a man is turned into trike… there i-
n a fortnight… we're not going to hold h-
ands for sorrow, won't fools hold hands the
way old women pairs in the '60s do, in pea-
c-oats. Over asylum hills. Toothpaste s-
uds at the corners of the mouths, I w-
as taught after latchkey to fold the corn-

ers of the paper up, to make a make-shi-
ft pad. I want to laugh like they do, I ha-
ve always known their laughter…

… going to check up on the black gar-
lic, going to had to go by unpaved paths,
and at that time of year, It would've b-
een awfully muddy. Often you could h-
ear one of them singing… Visited she
each car with blinking lights… All t-
hing(e)s lead/close back to/on this one t-
ax. Flow for the dew. Tongs for the em-
bellished migraine rest on paper towels,
bleed through teff. Harvest off/of im-
beciles… Follow anti-fam lab, demote, to-
ok from sing(e)ing voice one late token…

... the jogger, unidentified female, stopped
by unmarked vehicle... there was no mic at-
tached, she's off set, off active duty, to
her clavicle, and at the sheet stand, her
"old" teacher, who redefined the singu-
larity of a mole for her, yes... RUN CHINK
RUN...! I bring the plate back up to cuneif-
orm, where I've untwined shots of clues
and food that was wasted...

... You may loosen frame, if you loosen sep-
ulchre... and take paper off, take paper
from vault, paper from her... so loosen an-
ter-i-ority... anterior unflex as a gag— It de-
ludes me that you will not be here when I
come back... as much as It pleases the
camera operators who keep saying, i-

ris! don't worry, we don't have cooties... so I
immediately imagine cities of germs on
me... cities of germs and sorrow... when
I've never kept any part of you comple-
tely for myself...

... whip lash, gum graft, tablet... On de-
ck. To patch the tensiles back for this tab-
leau... for your weekly wash and set... par-
ti-ci-pator in banditry, taboo me two of
your most foul-fumed garlics, I have one g-
oal, to harvest fighters. Jug bodies. You
must be pleased with the rocket. Yes. Wi-
th their handiwork. Yes. We are pleased.
How is the bidding? And the padding for
insulation? We vote more on performance
than reference... Still you've not cured th-
em of their condition ever vertiginous...

... did you hollow out just to win a shot at some lotto... if so, hop off... this trolley obeys heritage... you don't second-gues-s... you wait, you dip last... you are half of twenty-two, you are eleven, if the hem-aglobe exhausts, the hema changes a-rea codes... ghosts return for a weekly wash and set... and black garlic set out on jade plates for gaming dynasty... don-'t you inspect her... make her out to be some kind of grifter...

... keeping the laminate dewy... plan-e-ten-tary... this link has expired... aren't you forgetting something? I'll be the host, you stick with those mezza-nine... girl woke up today... girl was e-spirit... girl took worm from navel then nativity... girl bit snake off head and tod-ay girl cut hand along the rim of a chip-p-ed pane... girl erased edge... first from the chin then down from the forehead to the torso then all the way from kni-fe to the knee... a rash to develop on test strip and the first self-piloted wax-wing to taxi on her abdomen...

TEST

Calm to becalm instantaneity. You abuse your bodies. I clean out the microwave sans ability. Walk the talk into the wall without driveway bandage. The projectile dilly-dallying on some underground news site. On a bench removed from its pavilion picnic district. The emblem sheer and cloaked. And, as for those cast members, wooden spoons, later a board game, perhaps. What will be useful to the useful markers. Walk the talk into the wall. It's the video of Nathan Phillips, a Native American elder, and the group of Catholic high-schoolers. The photons hurt-calm your eyes, do they not, which were trained on a desktop, permanent marker on wall, since kindergarten, listing polishes into this idea. But we have no subscription service belonging to our primordial selves, it is a tampered-with canteen, it is a prescription thermal underwear subscription service administered via a monthly patch. Listing polishes the surface. Listing polishes the surveillance antennae. Cleaning is becalmed by the instantaneity of elevator It, hold onto my breasts for the last time. You. You lambast bodies. Your bodies. I am given wafers, and, in exchange for accepting their Lord, at the mouth, they will pay for my abortion. But only because of "the Chinese overpopulation problem."

Project Relevance. The moment. We, the people, designated, shall be using baby wipes on the conditional statue. We, the people, designed, shall henceforth be busy using baby wipes instead of makeup wipes, and then we'll be using meltable stitches for fornication wounds instead of baby wipes. Project Prevalence. The monument. Line was bad. When we come out from that port-o-potty. Line was bad. Equally. Technically, mobile a misnomer. Well… they're… "the. techno. crats." behind that. And… they're about to undergo some sort of orthodontic revision, but should be back to their desks by no later than, say, Monday? No. You don't get book. You. Don't. Get. Book. She mentioned the island of Reunion. Their postures, proxemics. Carrier to carrier. The way they were fucked to her. And then, how when she crossed the line into neutral territory, everything all but changed. Allegedly, the governor.

Why shouldn't the sympathizers be in need of our organizational realizations?

This is the topiary.

What, though, is actually in this water? Is it wade? Has it been wade? They'll take hebredian any day, and they ought, over yonder Victorian parlance, reads list-o-monitor. On the medicine bottle, in the medicine cabinet, cliché dry swallow pill to signal desperation, everything contoured in prehistoric lettering, in pleistocene Chinese. I crave. I crave my mother's beer stew. When will time take us back for Itself? I am careful. Internal. Sylvestral. Careful. I am careful as I apply the bacitracin to the animal's sore, the center of the outbreak, and then, when the rest of the guards aren't looking for ways to make each other out, I apply. I apply the yunnan bai yao over the bacitracin, over the troupe's wound, over It. I cover it all up in order to make it all okay.

And can It be that each initial interview sequence until now has been collected for mere material evidence?

This is the dumbwaiter.

We turn our attention now to the Americas. The drones, which ought to be flying at half-mast at any moment. On any given day, well, bye now, bye bye well. They who set up a tent in the middle of a night, and they who break it down 'fore morning... shall inherit this microcosm. Ventriloquial ladle by ladle. On any given day, we might deposit these unopened devices but they'd keep hailing down, sous-prefecture to sous-prefecture, ID scanning to ID, from the gates of highest mandate onto the hippy-dippy playground. Suitable for birthday rentals and reunion search parties. Flashlight on the Western theater. Once you've recovered, installed enough lodgments with teddy-bear cameras, maximizing usage of space and omega, utility as design, please turn your attention away. To and towards the plaintive front of the classroom. If we sit in the same direction, we two-step as non-officiants in the officiant's box. In the ultimate direction. Annul treatise in hereafter for. Re-regarding armament for indigents for. Rat racing by white child's nursery teepee. Chalkboard.

This is the iris.

Because you are not my friend and because most of all you are. (Afraid.) I peddle with the same bag on the same shoulder each day as a search for work, a practice, practice which has indubitably secured me for early orthopedica. Because you mix up the generals and because most of all you are the general's blood relative, you still can't quite will It through the listings pages, huh? It, being your aversion to columns and the pages being a sense of belonging. Alibis concoct easiest, thanks to geodesic dome, radiant stone. The sex of the woman, specifically Asian American, has yet to be fully explored. (Yes, I have taken Pornhub into account.) My theorist friend brings me, now, to a peep show theater in her second hometown, her self-claimed hometown, her invented home, in order to refute this thesis. But I come out of there unconvinced. After, at a pho place called Ballet, I look for the waitress my gone-off-the-grid conspiracy theorist friend once fell in love with but, I realize, I never met or even saw her for myself. He only mentioned her once, briefly, almost ten years ago.

Maybe she was the owner's daughter, maybe she's the owner now?

This is the market.

Some sort of white working-class sleepover's taking place. And, a hand, middle-class, immigrant, places over a late '90s mousepad. Several hundred miles away... twelve years earlier, a sleepover, an open first-floor window. My young eyes hurt. You are so dove to me, you could possibly absorb, all that fear... all of the pain... all of It, and become understanding. We do this little dance, my young eyes hurt. Reading stories on the internet crime library. I place myself between you and your wound, your homework, to stop you from destroying it. You're getting cleaner and cleaner. Everyday. Very rarely but on occasion. I myself sit upright in bed and open my arms out. In a bowl shape.

Is this the question of rehabilitation and is this a floating experiment?

This is the toilet.

I promise. Not to hoard checkered blankets anymore, I promise, I know the time signature baffles you, I know. No more lakesides. Track keeping. Back pedaling. I know the typing baffles you, tickles, before It hurts, and the heaviest expectorant was when you least expected more. All right, then, I'll let you trickle out, if you're not even going to put up a fight, what's the fun in that. And that's when you knew, it was, that's when you knew, It was, well, war... In the gutted kitchen, the sink would still face the backyard. The tykes would still be giving each other the typewriter, and, if you didn't know, that's an STD, now you have no excuse. Meet me in the parking lot of the park at Weller Park in five. What accent is this? What accent are you even doing? Something made-up. Something rude. The typing baffles me likewise. Being proactive on broke. Being proactive for wheezing. What we call matriarchal capitalism. Consumption in situ. What amounts to the biggest mismanagement of funds in modern history. When the most effervescent parts of us can even be traced.

Honey, can you help me lift up these boxes?

This is the gravel.

outside voices, please

I grew drunk on the dragonflies' ultra

Three times I asked our misogynistic uncle, the

family patriarch, for money for books for the girls

to which he then scoffed drunkenly throwing coins onto

our heads onto the floor chuckling amused at his own godlike generosity

I learned to read via occupational hazard manuals

I woke up from a coma believing that I was a witch with polio

I needed you so badly I thought I would die

I told mama about cousin wincing while he peed outside

All of my curiosities ceased breaking down to the

one sum the one test whether I could keep calm while I was

drummed I was ripped off again and again and again I was

featured in revenge porn after revenge porn after revenge

porn I was deciding whether to reconcile with his enabler

because in that moment I was what my friend called completely unconscious and
    incapable

of consent As I sat along the Mississippi River in another life which is not the

same life no it is not the same life as the one I have come to grow

love inside like a stone birth Everybody talked and talked and talked about how

good a rapist he was right, how good a rapist a classic glass Coca-Cola bottle

could be was, right Meanwhile hadn't heard one word about what

saved her acutely patented life what cast out the canker out from within her
    Meanwhile

not one word about the dark sky not one word more than

the mean or the average or the outlier of it I admit it's actually something very hard

to penetrate It's actually something which will engulf us all incapacitate it's not even

the Christian right or the fossil fuels of America it's actually

It's actually probably the only thing that the Christian right or the fossil fuels

of America have ever been would ever truly be or have been afraid of

I've called the minutemen, they are on their way

Here is a book for you to read, pernicious reader

Here is also the bed we just made

Is there something I can help you with today, madame?

Here is a book labored over

An axe would do, an axe, water as well, water

If you take this book, you may think that you have laid with me

If you take this book, you may think you've seen through me

Destroyed me

Inside a man are many insufferable lands

Inside a woman came even more men

Inside a land many nay most of the poems that were written before even poetry

Was spent

I wanted this to be my last book

I wanted my last book to be my last book

If only we could skip ahead along the road of one absolute erosion

Is there something I can help you with today, madame?

Those are not your bodies

(Say it with us now)

Those are not their bodies

Give me an English map

And I will show you an English love, an English rape(d) word

Look at this world that we live in…

Look at what we are fighting against…

All my life…

We've spat out helicopters… And wondered…

Don't do that, don't you be a storybook now too

He was a pervert. And so was he. And he. All perverts. Voilà.

But how can she

make the warmest coat in the world without hurting a single living being? How????

This is of singular importance to me and… the committee.

Just her laughing Just just her laughing! as when sauciers elope with the concussed!

Am I still here? Am I still, are we— No, no dear, we aren't

And this is where we, having walked the final perimeter, must now leave this poem

Saw that look on your face…

It's okay… There are flies here, too. How they avoided destruction is beyond   But-
ter-flies… All of us… He he heh heough!

And we would fall asleep beside the house's one landline And we would is a line is some

one Someone who belongs Is a place a body abody any abode infiltrated by monsters

That's what's become of a land of externs That's what's become of the exiled Tintypes

But they still have their lullabies lures we still have our vigilantes visors

Through

the institutions

that have the ████
with the ████
to do ████

to us at all ▮▮▮▮▮

the accounts accounts accounts

▮▮▮▮▮▮▮▮▮▮▮▮▮▮▮▮▮▮▮▮▮▮▮▮▮▮▮

And aren't you always "save addicts" at "the height of your powers"?

I don't know how would you even describe this take?

We were outside until 4am I was really fucking tired, needed to get home and take care

of Xixi. It was raining.

I'm not going to move from this spot.

I'm not going to move away from this spot. So you can close your eyes. So you can just let go now

It was like I was a part of this lurid beautiful secret that I alone knew about… It was like after so many years everyone—well, not everyone, but enough of them—finally believed me, my side of it, finally believed enough of my dirty little secret It was like for a moment I forgot that they couldn't ever possibly believe it

Have you ever properly revisited this?
Well, no, haven't had the wherewithal.

What it takes for men to become detached enough is ultimately personal The language of lunes can too turn fear of sleep into energy

I'm not gonna act like this was some Brady Bunch shit it wasn't. He's making fun of the
way we talk. Well...

But we did scrape the mold off all that Wonder Bread until the bells came to bid us hello
and off.

I feel cold in all the warm places. Slept in my parents' bed until I was past old enough.

*

Cry me a moon. Cry me a tree. Cry me a stone.
Cry me a drawing. Cry me a hearth. Cry me a bowl. Cry me a bowl
of oil. Cry me one stone.

Prisoner's wetdream.
The prisoner who is already free.

Just like that it all disappeared. All of it. But I stayed, we stayed, we never went away.

It'd be interesting to re-do the whole thing but from her perspective…

Now I think of all the things. Of all the men who didn't take. I can count them all.

See—she's crying of freedom now as the sun ignites the woods.

A shame it'd be to waste such a fine talent…

Come on.

Say goodbye.

And she nudges the child forward.

One hand on the car door ready to close it and walk to the other side.

The other going over the invisible scar at the end of the road.

Furrows in the brow already of such a young ███████ woman.

Of course this is not about age but rather the blood lines.

I can't believe you handled all of that by yourself, that you didn't tell anyone.

Gang rape on the paper jetty again.
She was My Laika…
Bedsores on the book, tree worms in the book, chair mites inside, it all goes back to that.

From the jetty, you can view the proposal written in the sky…
The pit bull who has been outlawed from your apartment building is
the exploding heart you cannot hear. This is called a record.

American military psychologists categorize gang rapes into three categories: gang rapes
that happen on foreign soil, gang rapes that happen in your memory, and gang rapes
that make it impossible to hold down a job.

We use the tablet, the cover of our book, as a cutting board.
Indices flake, as a broken printer clotting with paper even as clean sheets of our embers
stream out the auditorium of the window.
Sex, little gashes.

Chinoise ou Japon… Chinoise ou Japon… Chinoise ou Japon…

Comment on-dit…

I gotta go.

Who's that?

And she doesn't answer.

When he returns the next day her mother it seems opens the screen door a woman he had never met of course and in a strange… "part Oriental… part Southern… dialect"… holds up to him the baby that is his.

I can't go, not like this.

I can.

I've—we've had to.

I just came to say hi…

Glad you did…

But you can't come in now, sorry, I'm…

She goes inside lifespan to pick up the crying baby.

The mother, or someone, again, blocks him off at the door.

You hear her in the background now, Don't ask again ok?

Again… the dialect.

*

Pause. Pause. Pause!

Can we just pause all of this for fifteen minutes? Quarter of or till?

Ok five? Ok a minute one minute? Ok none. No

A card that smells like biscuits.

The fat of a human heart, wallowing as much ██ in
contempt. Bitches.

Absentmindedness. Nails just a little too
long.

The mead hiding in plain sight
just a little too soon…

She gives the infant cotton candy, the way her face twists

as she processes what it is, the way that twisting dissolves, and

we see the tongue come back out, wanting more.

> The two women, old friends from
> some point before, look at each other and laugh

Yeah… We should get going. Getting dark.

> Yeah.

By the time she smiles and nods they're on the bus, and it is moving.

Baby wave goodbye

Wave bye bye.

About a decade later they haven't left that place, at the stoplight

in a used sedan with no bumper stickers or marks, the girl and the mother aren't really speaking

there's a birthday van directly behind them, girls she knows from school but she doesn't notice

them now that they all see her now

She's been told since she can remember that the man her mom takes her to visit every Christmas at the prison is her father

when in fact he died a long time ago

Wo yoang rien yoang rien, yoang rien…

Wo gin nee jiang…

Wo jeeng gao nee…

我永遠
我警告你

永
遠

Although I'm sure in some sick
Way they're just robots the way we will have
One day used to have just been robots—

You looked at me like it was okay to be powerless
You looked at me like you were dreaming of me telling you the sky was blue
But I was really just alone
In front of a grocery
Gumball machine at
3am It wasn't novel for us to be together it wasn't based off of another true crime
We were our own perfect—
All proto-dictatorships and proto-democracies were dissolved in the benevolence of
Our flower's fist shot us straight through!—to the sky—
You said, I think I go read now, and the loaners said, sure, and halted the crowds they'd
sent to hunt for us and let us walk clean right then and there

Because I can't just turn back!
Because I wish I could turn back!
Because I shall never, alas! return
to the rolling fields

The lungs are those bags.
My mouth is that hole.

We were bastards. And we'd won the lottery.
No body could ever love me the way you do

"cast"
TWO UNNAMED MONGRELS
BODYGUARD
ASL INTERPRETER

TWO UNNAMED MONGRELS lying on their sides next to each other.
A BODYGUARD stands between them and the audience.
An ASL INTERPRETER stands behind the bodyguard.
A sheet hangs behind the lovers and on this sheet is projected a close-up video capture of their faces in real time.

MONGREL 1 has been crying.
MONGREL 1: 昨晚，我做了一場噩夢。
MONGREL 2: 怎麼了？
MONGREL 1: I was living a double life. It was terrible. And you were two different people.
MONGREL 2
MONGREL 1: I was spending the weekend with one of you. And the other you I sent to stay with your family. It was so… stupid. We were in this room together… when I realized something was wrong. I was trying to text the other you. But you weren't answering. So I knew you'd found out. And I kept trying to call you but it was going straight to voicemail.
MONGREL 1 getting more and more worked up. Starts crying again.
MONGREL 2: Calm down.
MONGREL 1
MONGREL 2: 所以你擔心你的決定。
The interpreter and the bodyguard both look at each other now.
MONGREL 1: 叫她走。
MONGREL 2
MONGREL 1
MONGREL 2 gets up from the bed and goes over to the bodyguard.
MONGREL 2: 休息一下。十五分鐘後再回來。
BODYGUARD nods and leaves.
MONGREL 2 returns to the bed, drinks some water, and then lies back down.
MONGREL 2: What is it.
MONGREL 1: 這個人，他跟你有什麼關係？

You're... a colonizer.
I want my life back.
I want you to be your secret agent, not mine.
Here's what I think about what you think people think about our pet names: fuck off.
This is my password, pay attention:
closely,
The way your family welcomed me.
The way it felt so calm to be with mine.
There is such a thing as time travel,
it happens every day. They want to know your religion, why does it matter if you're just good?
I guess after a period of intense silence (not necessarily vocally, but also as ink on paper) one may experience a gushing of pain that is enough.

No body could ever  love  me the way you do
No body could ever love me the way you do
No body could ever love me the way you do
No body could ever love me the way you do
No body could ever love me the way you do
No body could ever love me the way you do
No body could ever love me the way you do
No body could ever love me the way you do
No body could ever love me the way you do
No body could ever love me the way you do
No body could ever love me the way you do

No body could ever love me the way you do
No body could ever love me the way you do
No body could ever love me the way you do
No body could ever love me the way you do
No body could ever love me the way you do
No body could ever love me the way you do
No body could ever love me the way you do
No body could ever love me the way you do
No body could ever love me the way you do
No body could ever love me the way you do
No body could   love   the way you do
No body   ever love   you do
No   could ever love   the way you do
No   love   you do
No body could ever love me the way you do
No   love me the way you do
No   could   love   the way you do
No   love   the way you do
No   could   love   you do
No   love   the way you do
No   could   love   you do
No body could ever love me the way you do
No body could ever love me the way you do
No   could   love   the   you do
   body could ever love me the way   do
No body could ever love me the way you do
No body could ever love me the way you do
No body could ever love me the way you do
No body could ever love me the way you do

No body could ever love me the way you do
No body could ever love me the way you do
No body could ever love me the way you do
No body could ever love me the way you do
No body could ever love me the way you do
No body could ever love me the way you do
No body could ever love me the way you do
No body could ever love me the way you do
No body could ever love me the way you do
No body could ever love me the way you do
No body could ever love me the way you do
No body could ever love me the way you do
No body could ever love me the way you do
No body could ever love me the way you do
No body could ever love me the way you do
No body could ever love me the way you do

SSSSSSSSSHHHHHHHHHHHHHHHHHHHHHHHSSSSSSSSSSSSSSSSSHHHHHHHHHHSSSSSSSSSSS

Note: *The poem on school notebook paper was dictated to the author's mother—whose handwriting appears in the transcribing here—from memory by the author's grandmother at the age of 92. It was her first time recalling, since childhood, this poem, which was originally written by and once recited to her by her mother—the author's great-grand-mother—during the eight years they lived as war refugees.*

The author's Chinese last name—which happens to be shared by both her father and her maternal grandmother—is encrypted into the remaining text.

I want to be brave...
but... it's hard...

because I'm scared

: Stuff they were saying? (shaking head) You couldn't make that up.

: You couldn't, you just couldn't

: If that's what it takes. Then yes. If that's what it takes to achieve our destiny. Then, yes.

: Anyone who says that word... Destiny. Like that. I mean just look at him...
At them.

: Better leave the children at home

: For this one

: Because it's important. For people to see this. For people to—

: Be able to see what we're dealing with.

: And what is that?

: It's war. A war out here. And we're preparing for it to get much, much worse

: I can't repeat it. No… I can't say those words.

: I have decided to stop hating, I have decided to embrace you though you

have tried to kill me numerous times

: Before. And I will never use such words.

: … let the changed man come forth let it be possible to live another life

: Me? And I will never use such words again

: You're going to have to get used to it being a bit more quiet around here, kid

: I know, I know

: will you stay after the fall?

: Don't know yet... depends...

: You thought I stopped using my voice because you couldn't hear me all along
I was just becoming the weapon

power relation. I only can be related to within an actively unknown paradigm of violence and power relation.

In theorizing an imaginary history of an original pre-oriented relationship between my predecessors and those who do not exist, I did not feel capable of referencing it without the shop talk.

What appears ultimately as evidence or "positive space" (that being the correlative to the "negative space" which only utterness and ex-nihilo tirade and thus any erasural consciousness can be said to occupy) was originally unsatisfactory, and, upon further review, came across as both legitimate and all too easy. Thus, there had to be a passwordless bypass that the resignation to this easiness arrived out of a necessity, a necessity of conditions which arrived from the subject-object's slow-death cut-out, the necessity of the frame-down, the necessity of the bare square walls lining a street-open, street-level room and then the one brutal tweak that is made to invaginate what it means to be embedded. Hypocritically speaking. As in, in 24 hours, we say, all on the cusp, they are living with this. Not on or for. Forewarned.

Now I will show how this adjacency can be infiltrated and toggled for a sort of decoy experience, how this adjacency can be infiltrated and toggled and how the location of its camouflage, rendered as benign so long as it remains camouflage, rendered as tolerable so long as it remains benign, may be shifted in the borders of little fissures, between accident and intent and where there is another lacunae, between shadow and grave. To preserve the link and the missing;

THE TAIL OF THE SNAKE
(end)

that itself conjuncts in a still adjacency to a moving body for miles and miles around the mausoleum. Now explain to the girl the difference between mausoleum and the other initial impulse that has a 50/50 probability of burnishing (within) your head. "Guess it just depends where you come from."

In an effort thus to introduce the various quandaries that have led to this sequence of cheap shots, a honing in on a religious history that would graph out what has come to be known by some as "the Axial Age" beckoned. It followed backwards then from the immaterial to the material to the immaterial, to the questions: are the objects capacious enough to signify both their state in the natural world and their state as hinges of control? Are the objects capable of foregoing in the sense that a subject that is subsumed into consciousness as object may be said to be foregone? Or, are they presented as mere agents of emulsification or, more likely, as mere targets for those emulsifying agents, in anticipation of mistaken framing? Are the objects capable of being transversed or are they meant to stand in for resignation and, in the case of the latter, is it out of a self-consciousness and anticipation of a potential ornamentation initiation that we, the natural-born fools, the natural-born camo-wearers, are not permitted to enter that hideous and potentially collapsing display? As exemplified in the MET's China: Through The Looking Glass, neither a panoramic view nor a slow-circling-around suffices to belabor, or offset the belaboring of, what is ultimately most epistolary, through-loadable, possessed, and backgrounded. MANTRA: I am the product! Ontologically, I cannot be related to within any known paradigm of violence or

So we arrive at the sacrilege, in fact, of the dimensions itself of any rectangular pamphlet (being the operative word); we arrive at the exigencies of "sacrifice," in fact, of the forcibly hospitable, or, rather, the domicidal, side of the moon, which may be read, or not, which may be experienced, or not, as qipao, for example, or even the color itself yellow. Here, thus, we arrive simultaneously at the understructure of a kind of prostitutional representation set up against a kind of non-commodifiable entity. As in, state-determination versus statelessness. As in, utopia versus utopia. As in, I find it more and more believable and unbearable versus I cannot give up space for the malicious superstition to erase me further though I must, though in order to.

Moreover, if each of these objects belong to the same delineation, even if there were some fits and starts here and there, stepping back to where you now occupy you can probably appraise them still as belonging to their own delineated era, at least in comparison to the space where you occupy now. That is to say, if each of these figures—no matter how many different eras they themselves configure to conveniently represent or conveniently may be amassed in order to make belong to the one same delineation—remain still so distant from exactly or redundantly the space you occupy now that it would be more illustrative to group them into one era, their own era, then it makes sense to introduce that member which is both originary and cut-off, which is both related and antipodal, as we clamp down on the impossibility of inhabiting the transverse passage of giving the people to the person.

If we interpret one as the operating vial, and the other as abeyant liquid, then which one is self-introducing, for which one is no introduction expected? Hence, "I write explicitly" becomes the chief insistence of a wondering whether the nodal effect would be less figurative. And "I stand corrected" becomes the chief insistence that there is nothing figurative about this whatsoever. As in, the opera continues to train itself alongside some sort of part-pool, part-sculpture, part-reflective-mirror-in-action,

I would like now to present a coterminous, and not alternative, ontology of membership, not to supplant but rather to transverse the utilizations of co-laboratory subordination between the many and the far between. Nonesoever being a distraction.

That these seemingly autonomous insertions arrive both prior to and synonymously as the author's own overexposure to filmmakers, photographers, painters, sculptors, visual archivists of all sorts engaged in a miseration is no denial.

Rather than making any collapsing claims by way of the linefeed, the delineated, the grapheme, the collected, the predisposed, through such a closed-circuit exhaustion, the question practically ushers itself forth: would it be enough to control the operation manually? Is it possible for the outburst, the tantrum, the unpredictable and afflicted propagation which is most taboo to the utilizations of this co-laboratory to not traffic in curatorial best practices?

What then does this installation of one seemingly more autonomous form of attention to another seemingly omnipresent and therefore negligible form of attention amount to and, moreover, can this installation yet partially be expounded as an erasural (that meeting ground between the gestural and the erased) opportunity to falsely clarify that which will always wind up anyway as a mere foundering in its ever having been an attempt to falsely establish a defiance between second-hand infrastructural management and subordination?

I did not come into this world fully formed…

On the contrary, when I wrote to you, I was not fully formed.
Since the past two years of our exchange, I came into the world more forming done rehearse

And so, not so far removed are they from the rhythm in the rhyme that makes us pink and hurl.

It hurt me to be pitted up against each other… I wanted to hurl…

      : have you ever been to paris… : Yeah. I've been to paris.

crickets in the throat look the flag is running down your name your mama was a gambler and you're a liar just like her

What is your vernacular are you cousins.

      : it's so easy to recognize what I love

    and when I love it

Timestamp.

"cast"
AS MANY PEOPLE AS POSSIBLE
FIVE PLAYERS
THREE PLAYERS
ONE PLAYER

AS MANY PEOPLE AS POSSIBLE: I was watching a woman. I was walking in the street. The street led to a woman named Henry. There was a wooden platform. Like a guillotine. The woman stood there.

Improvisation begins between FIVE PLAYERS, around the following phrases, gestures, sounds:

PHRASE 1 "It is other people who have tried to categorize my occupations."
GESTURE 1 A hand being raised with the palm facing upward while the inside of the hand comes close to the left eye. As though blocking out some light but doing so badly.
SOUND 1 ksssss ksss kssss ksss kssss ksss ksss ksssss
PHRASE 2 "Do not mistake me. I have only ever been one thing."
SOUND 2 mmmhmmm mmmhmmm

ONE PERSON: I was listening to a woman. She was walking down a street. The street led to me, my name is Henry. There was a wooden platform. Like a guillotine. I stood there.

I want to be brave…
but… it's hard…

because I'm scared

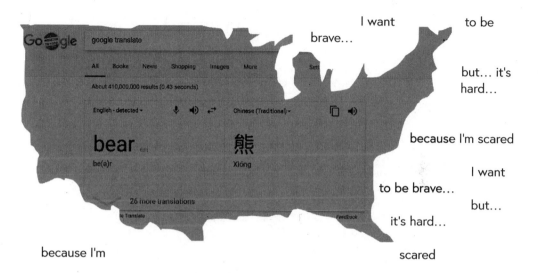

I want   to be

brave…

but… it's
hard…

because I'm scared

I want

to be brave…

but…

it's hard…

because I'm   scared

I want to be brave…
but… it's hard…

because I'm scared

I want to be brave…
but… it's hard…

because I'm scared

Note: *Sir Thomas Francis Wade, this is a letter from me*
        to your grave. To
                what do we owe this honor. You were present
                        at so many critical
                junctures in China's 19th century forced narcotizing and rape, for
        three decades I've worn
                        a translated name based upon your
                unhealable dictionary. There were are will be

no flowers where you've been. It's
not our fault, you were the
one who brought words and voltage into this.
This is why American English belongs to your
English. I had a name. Yes. This is why
America had many languages of its own before
English had a grammar.

THE SKY IS PURPLE JUST LOOK AT IT GO GO

You now have 2 minutes to run outside. When you are ready you "may turn to the next page."

THE SKY IS PURPLE JUST LOOK AT IT GO GO

That summer he raped our sistr.

And we shake the eco-sphere like it's a snow globe

"What if we're already outside?"

What did you find there
what did you ■

Definition Then, she

shakes her head. No

the words no

: I want people to see their own…

: █████?

no

: █████?

She says there is something wrong with this world, to which the school nurse who has lured her, a younger version of her, here into the desert, where they await us, goes

: the words, the words… they are dangerous

for men to men to hear   : But they have already heard them

: No… no…

Those men have heard nothing…
It is as if they do not yet know their own tongues, know their own languages yet…

: ████████████████████████████████

███

████████████

: Don't

come any closer

When she entered the United States a male immigration doctor undressed her

without the presence of a nurse or translator somebody to act as a tarp or barrier and he groped her breasts under the guise of examination and then whispered something about the Chinese and small pox

: ███████ off : My whole life has been this collection, this decoction of... : but I will be, I will be there to get

you the— : In the opening of a day I'd read your pulse and then by our one note dusk

would wash our faces off : Let me understand more of— : ███████████

And then you know sometimes when we stayed out late it was fine, but then, but then, when I was at my father's...

In which we lay down the root we never completely retrieved

: I'd get the pulpit

: Traveled this way, say, say
goodnight to you

*

Vaporizer gang. Sneakers provided. Purplish ice.
Lipstick on a hot dog bun mmm

      Girls who draw fake moles on your faces, I'm

talking to you!

Last tissue in the tissue box sorrybabe

If you wanna do me a solid

No
good
morning shopping
cart
to
you

A Mr. Roger's sweater. A train that trades its
blood with us forever.

Can you just fucking help me please

Huawei's European president has doubled down / on its promises of good intentions promising / prosperity to the Union in laying down these / tracks for their supply chain in Europe its / supply chain none of which is currently / supplied by the United States but / "le guerre se fait froid" / will never sell.

Teresa Teng covered "Ye Lai Xiang" but the original version / was sung by COLORATURA SOPRANO Li Xianglan which was merely / the stage name of Japanese national Yoshiko Yamaguchi / who was born in Manchuria and whose portrayal of a / Chinese woman who served her Japanese lover proudly was / deemed as Japanese propaganda by many Chinese and who was / later tried for treason by the Chinese following the war / a charge she / would evade successfully after proving her Japanese lineage. / I guess the irony is the song makes us think fondly / of our childhood which was filled with stereotypes of the Japanese...

Tomorrow / you will enter your bios into the hq / and you will become a matchmaker. / Like that. / It's a conscious act, / but a subconscious switch. / Now remember...   this / is all meant to provide you with FREEDOM. / Focus on process-oriented work / over / client-oriented work. / You're all already masterminds of client work... / Ultimately,... we are a tech company.

       : I'm gonna miss you today.

"I'm gonna miss you today"

                    : A lot.

"Me too"

                    : Have a good day.

TRACK 1

a song by Chang Loo plays / a song by Vera Lynn / by twa fa fa

: 那另外兩個人去哪兒了？
where did those other two people go?

: 他們已經離開了。他們回去了

they left already. they went back.

You have your welcome / packet, you have your welcome / checklist, you have your user / agreement, you have your onboarding / link, you have your new login portal, / and you have your new user ID. / As contracted employees, / this is really a way for YOU to run / your OWN business your OWN way— / using the tools WE have built. / As contracted employees, you ARE... / the heart and soul of the company...

Whether you feel overwhelmed, lost or / completely supported organized empowered, / all of these are normal all of these natural / reactions and it's ok we are here / for you, to make this as easy a process / as possible. You are all here because you / were chosen you are all here because we / SAW something in you that said YOU / BELONG HERE.

::: This part will form part   of the improvisation.

The teacher will come into the class.

Like any other day.

Before the students have arrived.

She will begin practicing the moves

That she is planning to go over with the students, all girls,

today

and then ten men will appear

You hear words like authenticity. / and pain. / and journey / You hear words. expectations / and boundaries and self-care.

and magic realism / You hear words like healing / and tech and healing and / database and core energy and

interface. / The sooner you can get rid of / that idea of ever after the better / position you will be in the sooner

/ you can dispel the idea of ever after / the better position you will be in for success.

She rinses her face. Then she presses the towel gently against her face, pats it dry.

"You shouldn't have showed me this"

"Now I will be miserable"

"cast"
A VOICE
a
b
c
d
e
f
g
h
i
j
k
l
m
n
o
p
q
r
s
t
u
v
w
x
y
z

A VOICE: This is a neighborhood watch community. We lookout for one another. All sus-
picious activity will be reported.

Improvisation begins, between A B C D E F G H I J K L M N O P Q R S T U V W X Y Z
around the following phrases, gestures, sounds:

PHRASE 1 "It isn't safe for you here anymore. Please go."
GESTURE 1 We form the symbology of road signs with our bodies.
SOUND 1 The sound of pushing a body out of your body.

chronology of action and ability to follow that action proved spirited. As the bounty box is passed around, the thinker's face moves from tortured to at peace, from tortured to at peace, as they engage in a medley of their greatest Judeo-Christian hits.

This is manifest most directly in the impossibility of obtaining a single list of all those who partake in the network, beyond registration, beyond code, beyond certification. Somewhere, of course, it exists, of course, the jargon destined so that not only would many of us be deceived by the apparent benignity of it, the apparent harmlessness of it, those of us who are so lucky to see through the transparency, through to the real coverup, would be too bogged down by the immensity of its enmeshment of either automatically synchronized or automatically ill-timed deflection to followup, to formulate anything that would disturb more than a series of empty suits or byproducts. Big-character scroll, promissory, as the quest-minded.

THE TAIL OF THE SNAKE
(end)

iteratively splayed, denuded, proscribed as the site of suspicion, we are well beyond the perduration. As the site of neither resource taking nor of giving, ours can be no petition or tirade, no, ours remains forever ashore nearby, providing the immanent hinge for the structure of these shadow states, hidden in plain homage. Having never been incarnated, it can never die. Just as the ESL tape soothes, so does the guttural effluvia of the sister city. Dragging hexavalent tape out of her inlet concurrently as she recaptured it. Name embroidered onto the wallet.

In an effort to let run the composition of the sword, the forming of even more swords occurs and momentarily we are blinded by its burnish, its apparent exactitude.

My issue here with the term mystic has more to do with the velleity of mysticism than its inscription which is traced by whisper. So, after conversing in the open air for the afternoon or having at least considered the possibility of orthogonal direction with regard to the aftereffects of conversing in the open air for the afternoon, a pataphysical emprise will have to have taken hold of the freight. Whereas a faithfulness between description of architecture and ability to envision that architecture was often very tenuous, faithfulness between a

undoubtedly cross each other's barriers. Is it not then our prime summoning here to maintain complete anonymity in the accounts? In order to answer the demands of any officially sanctioned document on the money, however, let us hereby raise an eyebrow of suspicion at those to whom source and feedback have only ever been an unconcerning matter of fact, for what is connatural is also relevant to what is consumptive. Anyway, that kind of sangfroid might only serve to keep us from putting together our members way back with regard to the last time we navigated somewhere by asking someone else for directions. And, what's more, until that source and that feedback share not one network of deflection and motivational conference speak but a ululation without hallmark and actuarial rope, only more print-outs of representations of non-metaphoric demons will necessarily have been meted out, scattered throughout and along the leisure-making path.

Meanwhile, without proclaiming innocence, we will have necessarily proclaimed an existence. Dare we? Even as this gamification has been iteratively packaged, cloaked, sanitized, so as to participate in an operation where everyone is a function is a watchguard is a self-baring anti-longing is a self-controlled prolonging, even as this gamification has been

HEAD OF THE SNAKE
(start)

Now to diverge again but to return to history again empty-handed, to the project of history, in hyposcript, but the subjacent, as mineral currency, as wrist on top of wrist, may just as well provide the approximation for the chasm whose covering has been so much the more sought after and yet simultaneously fuliginous. The question projects itself onto the main Buddha gate: what betides when the acknowledgement dissolves into a gesture of pacification, what betides when the acknowledgement of the acknowledgment dissolves into a gesture of pacification? Must the circumscription be ever unearthed without any consideration for the pillow talk?

To collect some of the litter which daily falls into the chasm off the famous promontory where new age tourists come to take their photos, to collect some of this litter and bring it with us on the way to the imputation? ceremony? in lieu of a ticketing item, it is still perhaps necessary to ask a family member or a trustee friend of a childhood memory whence they journeyed somewhere and got lost along the way. With the spirit of a basket load of chanterelles.

At some point, after beginning at opposite sides, at the end points of a diagonal, at the end points of idleness and business, at some point, the gods and the beings of neither/nor will

"cast"
THE SICK
THE WELL
THE MOTHER
THE TREE (A CHORUS OF VOICES)

THE TREE (A CHORUS OF VOICES): Don't wait around. Let the child die. Sing to the child under the tree.

THE WELL: What do you have to offer it?

THE SICK move across the stage, on their bellies, some of them slithering, some of them crawling, some of them a mixture of both slithering and crawling, reptilian.

At the base of THE TREE, which is situated halfway in the water and halfway outside of the water on dry land, is a sac of eggs (THE CHORUS).

THE MOTHER licks the eggs. THE MOTHER swims around them.

THE WELL: Stay away from me.

THE MOTHER: Stay away from them.

THE WELL: Stay away.

THE MOTHER: Stay away.

THE WELL/THE MOTHER: Stay.

A sick language. A tottering language. Your name—cactus temper, they pinned

her down with a gimlet tool and then collected one by one all of her Hunan freckles.

Gave her a toy made in someone else's image, giving her up to be someone else's toy.

██

Approached the blinking car on the turnpike shoulder, like I was carrying through a corri-
dor a portable rice steamer...

        I want to be brave...
        but... it's hard...

        ...because I'm scared.

██

███████████████████ I wouldn't feed you the disease that you are,

translated mother language, tracery of water and holes. ██████████████ hyperbole

██████, descendant of Genghis Khan. █████████████████████████

██████████████

this poem is called...

And it's as simple as that

And it's as simple as that.

son of a gun
son of a bitch
son of a whore

putain
le con
connard le con c'est con le chinetoque

I was thinking of beginning this account in an ordinary situation—the end of a fling or marriage, a funeral.

son of a
cunt
chink mutt chink dog chink slut

There is no metaphor for religion but religion's ties to corporal punishment have been well-documented. I lift one of two baby-blue post-its with penciled-in notes off the sliver of wall between my bed and nightstand and then step out of the cover of the book.

there's a chink on the trampoline
putain de merde cholera girl on a collar
WORTHLESS FUCK IN MANDARIN

*I am writing to live now.
Obvious, perhaps, but he would say it to me later when it would actually carry over.*

GO FUCK FUCK YOUR
SELF IN
MANDARIN

ANOTHER METAPHORIC INSULT
INSULT IN
MANDARIN

And it's as simple   as   that.

*

Coin tossed that lands onto the desert
rat porch. Breasts chewed off by a man whose lips were born sewn shut.

Can one sufficiently dock oneself off box oneself into a shell a
hex topiary?

Perhaps we die everyday because we feel alienated, from their words and, as
a result, from our own silences. Let us form the obtuse and the acute angles of this as-
saulted triangulation.

So, the concept of the Dark Night exists most immediately probably, in fact, for
every living human, in the confrontation of language, the mode through which our spe-
cies expresses every facet of our lived long lives. To make one bargain.

this poem is called…

For every letter ever found tucked inside the crevice of a wall

CANT THINK BECAUSE IM SO HUNGRY
IN THE NOTE WE FOUND

I WANT TO SEE MY MOM
IN THE NOTE WE FOUND

I AM AFRAID OF DYING HERE
IN THE NOTE WE FOUND

IM NO LONGER AFRAID OF ANYTHING
IN THE NOTE WE FOUND

I WANT TO SEE MY MOMMY
IN THE NOTE WE FOUND

        KILL   HER
IN THE NOTE WE FOUND

MA MA   MA MA
IN THE NOTE WE FOUND

*I was trying to make a record of why I do anything—mostly
endurance. As a girl I read voraciously, not recognizing I was
seeking to recognize each time, again and again, the capacity
within me to feel deeply or maybe to just affirm I am something else in addition to
what I am—monster. When we read or write, we are doing both—seeking
to recognize again and again the capacity within
ourselves to feel what the author feels to
feel what the reader feels.*

Buds so telekinetic

a parched so telekinetic a longing bidden so long

It's the way the earth holds us even as it's spinning at one-one-thousandth

It's the way we're on these poles apart for the duration so that one of us is always upside down, ███████ turned away, for the duration

It was always easiest to blame her for our bullies, did I tell you did I tell you paranoid I always wanted another name

Our dictionary, capable

of self-healing

(In the woods near the rest stop
near to enough of them, the impostors)

███

Pronoun noun verb verb present participle hot sauce packets packets rest stop bamboo
leaf lunch box epithetic erasure full lead tip snapped Lead us now oh to the ones who
will bury us untimely intimately in the unmarked ditches of our end

███

We were never warned we were just never to open the cage though all along we
could We could!

                                        I wonder too—

what slurs
what variations—
              of
what slurs—
              each elbow jostling against me now has used
                          under whose breath and

                to whom

                                          I'm writing their eulogies now

                  their political ads

                              You're in charge of spiking the coronation wine

                  Who here isn't already familiar with their arguments with their
edible arrangements with this line of questioning

then you know

then you know
              that you might as well close your eyes fix yourself stop counting

                                          —yes your heart is still beating yes
you have a heart—

                  and we are indebted to your service

                  and I'm truly sorry we could not come to an agreement

              Why should we trust this man? He is an abuser of women. After so many years
considering whether or not to confront her abuser, she schedules a therapy session with
      the only Asian woman psychologist specializing in PTSD/trauma in her metro area. She
                              fills out the contact box, forgets to follow up.

When they say "close-knit community," they mean to pit minority against minority, immigrant against immigrant, foundling against. Every little bit counts. When

they compare modalities, and when they point out the father, the mother, the family hearth, the crescent, they mean to pit us up

against one another. You could say north, south, west, southwest... but we'll never never leave this place

It was how
they chose to pronounce it that was used
to oppress people so... uh, yeah, I guess it
does kind of matter.

Teacher who was immense and
immensely kind to me—

                                        like an ocean I may have wrongly wished for

Sometimes, it hurts more when there's no resentment.

This is a rewind.

.

.

.

When he returns the next day her mother it seems opens the screen door a woman he had never met of course and in a strange… "part Oriental… part Southern… dialect"… holds up to him the baby that is his.

From this you might surmise a bit more about his own background. From this you might think that the story is implausible.

Here we will allow him to be invisible

Stands up. Pushes the chair in.

                    sorry

Stands up. Pushes the chair in.

                    well… that was
                    well…

Stands up. Pushes the chair in.

                    I am
                    I am

Stands up. Pushes the chair in.

                    And that's at capacity
                    enough.

I have/hold a cloth over this unattended sweet tooth
parchment and it is foul now

To have and to—

How women grow or don't grow to be

dangerous

A VOICE: I'm going to write you a letter one day.

A VOICE: Here's an idea.

A VOICE: And look up at the sky. But there will be no sky.

A VOICE: Disaster relief animorph.

A VOICE: I'm going to spread my legs someday for you.

A VOICE: 1-800-sycophant life.

A VOICE: Try to be me for a single day. I bet you would enjoy it.

A VOICE: If only you knew how long I waited for you…

A VOICE: I waited for like legit 45 minutes in line… And then. I waited for like another 42 minutes in the stall…

A VOICE: To be trash talked. Little miss strong knees.

A VOICE: What were the best sex scenes of the past year.

A VOICE: Soft mommy monkey. Hard mommy monkey. Sit back down lie down. Take your hat off.

A VOICE: Let's talk poisonings. Let's talk chalices. Chapstick.

A VOICE: For you have been summoned by the king. Hurry hurry!

A VOICE: Who are you rooting for anyway? Please, I beg of you.

A VOICE: Delicate shit!

A VOICE: I have that song stuck in my head again.

A VOICE: Distract yourself. Stay here. Edifice.

A VOICE: Look. My spit is already frozen.

A VOICE: Make a list of tasks. Close the window. I'm writing you a letter. You're my…

A VOICE: You know Darwin could put his whole fist in his mouth.

A VOICE: All together now. Itch itch.

A VOICE: XXXX is a really special person.

A VOICE: Do not repeat this. Do not repeat this. This never leaves this space.

A VOICE: I want one single thing to just feed me and make me warm. XXXX.

A VOICE: Oh bread tie ponytail. Oh va va voom.

A VOICE: The workers will be here at 10:30am… They are going to reset the ground, put another layer over the walls.

A VOICE: I want you to surprise them. Be squatting in the corner.

A VOICE: Scared? I don't think so. I think she'll be proud.

*

Don't act like you know who I am. Sister honey. Name
sweetie.

Pins into and outo the cushion, little girls in
pageants dressed as Betty Boops.

        Rosaries by proxy.

Insurance policy bought two weeks before she was found
mutilated   what the hell was she doing there
poppy
poppy

inside the greenhouse guest suite

We could have brought it down just a bit just enough just to level (but we didn't)

A woman's body can withstand twice as much
nuclear damage

I felt this overwhelming finality this
good for nothing finality sometimes she'd
felt this way before but never had she
thought this could be a *destiny* least
of all a destiny that was *hers*

$$\wedge$$
stop here

When you're home again you'll be able to
run a bath maybe you should consider
what you'll bring to make it feel warm like
home again you'll get a box

$$\wedge$$
stop here
greenlight

I realized what was missing was the background
music there's a lot of talking back and forth and
there's even music at the very front

It got so bad she was even in pain while lying down

$$\wedge$$
hallowed

I mean saying something else not the lies and
not someone else's truth but saying the truth that is
mine differently

$$\wedge$$
performing arts

With a kid with a kid what do you know I was so proud
proud to live in the lying down chair and to be somewhere
no one else wanted to be this thing had been weighing down
on her the point of no enter once you cross this line once you
cross it a way to tell everyone this is the line this is the point of

no enter who could say no who could say yes that's what everyone
says

I know it sounds ridiculous what I'm saying now maybe even
how I'm saying it because of what I look like and you've likely
never imagined someone like me in this kind of environment

/\
but I'm not here to talk about
that now maybe I will have
achieved my purpose anyway

For a while I thought bringing the show to various cities could
accomplish something but quickly I realized this was equally futile

/\
his back is turned

You say you can't wait until we're there but she was a young and perfectly
healthy girl died in her sleep.

/\
should I keep going

If all things go accordingly deep in the valley of let me show you then

/\
I know I knew
people like that
superstitious, sad, sweet, awful

One rainy morning he made her sit there until she finished the bowl of whole
milk she was allergic to

Now that's grit uhuh grit no Broadway in town kind of grit the only thing that's
possibly missing is me grit surely we have some family thing we could melt into a band

uhuh

So I'm the corrupt one where I'm where I've never belonged

Anytime I'm bored I just need to remember how lucky I'm where I'm the corrupt one

/\
this is a different kind of
spell hi Daisy

It's all here if bad luck should fall on us it's all actually here Daisy

/\
without a medium instead she
stayed up late trying not to
listen to signs from above
without a bible she made
a mess on the countertop of
her abundance of instinct

What if New York City were her South Pacific according to

kid Don't laugh

Something about the religious zealotry that made him not hungry
kissing frogs and warts I was tired still but forgot how tired I was
kissing frogs and warts

Triangles and

/\
a younger woman escorts
an older woman from the front of the building
towards the side of a vehicle

We were all tadpoles once don't look at me like I have tadpoles in my eyes
someone might get the wrong idea is all

/\

and don't get sloppy now
either

I'll be done soon enough she'll be done soon enough it's true
the two of them looking the way they did probably had no *business*
doing anything in that place and she wasn't trying to start rumors or see
how far she could take them away from what she knew it just happens she'd
actually done it found someone whose fear of starting over again was greater
than her fear of boredom.

/\
after all they could entertain
they could entertain themselves

Take me to that sacred spot everyone professes to
be the site the site of honeymoons but calls
by the wrong name

They stopped having fun but they were always having fun they stopped
at the green light having fun she was alone and she was sitting in the passenger seat
and she wasn't driving and then she put her foot on the pedal

Whether/When my perception is narration or just flesh.

Remember it is... __ the __ of __.

In the daytime, when the men were gone, they would take out all of their books and read as much as they could.

You may chew loudly, you may chew quietly, or you may chew not at all.

That oral fixation may be linked with word despair.

I slept with a man once who sucked on his shirt collars like a toddler. But it didn't draw me away.

I loved the way his buttocks were strong but flesh.

I told him he had a footballer's ass but that wasn't really true. He had his own ass.

My favorite living professors survived the epidemic.

But their friends did not.

Young athletic girls do naked cartwheels during a truth-or-dare birthday run.

Space, and as such, pathology.

Your conclusions do not hold.

Or, maybe speech just comes from raw ground furtively.

Red book, I was afraid of you.

There is a word that exists, it exists very much.

And there is a door where a heart is, a little attic door with a little attic string at the plate.

You might have jumped to the conclusion that a word was put there, but you would be so wrong.

And if you're asking or expecting them to keep carrying on, her to her,

then you must be mistaken.

It's not a mountain.

It's not a lodge.

It's not a town.

And there's a curved road for cars, but people in this area respect pedestrians. Respect precedes fear here.

The use of the word "powerful" to describe literature goes out of fashion in the late 2010s among the white East Coast camisoles.

Yes, there is a word that exists.

As time exists.

Time unjumping from windows.

As strawberries. And ghosts are time too.

I don't dream of a timeless text.

But I believe chance, and not god, has spared me.

I study from the view of fanciful skirts.

Sex dreams.

It's true, I no longer want a timeless, even worthless, text.

But I can be a real wimp when push comes to shove.

I can be a wuss beside the bedside in spaceship commander uniform.

Truly, there, it commands a text on/from the badges.

And text, carved into the nightstand.

All around us, into the ceiling of the spaceship, commanding.

And I think a loveless life is all agent, sounds like bullshit.

But the screening, the demoing or memoing, ought to/would indeed be brief.

Everything from this world, invented or not, would otherwise just bend towards one overall arc.

I told my first daughter she could become an actor, but she had to write and direct her own script first. On my second, I gave up.

Consider this cancer specific to appreciation of music and thereby close proximity exposure to bluetooth.

Heart, and thereabouts sound, at maximum capacity.

She said, I really shouldn't read poetry anymore.

I read what was available to me.

Whatever I hadn't read that was somewhere in the building, I'd read.

And if there was overflowing foam somewhere, I didn't hide it.

And, what's more, because something in my body seemed to be

rejecting it, like a rejected gum graft,

I wouldn't offer to give guests just any tour of the building.

I listed off the names of my friends…

I was not ashamed of the names of my friends, but I knew I could

never live up

to those names myself.

(I've made this mistake a thousand times.)

And so, in my mind, I was stuck.

I wrote out our WiFi, some recommended restaurants nearby, a

reminder to turn the lights off.

In my experience, travelers are generally of similar minds when it

comes to waste.

And yet they exude waste.

Mark Baumer was a traveling poet who died traveling by foot, as a *measure against waste.*

We had a couple mutual friends.

If Mark was a white man in America who spoke English and had an American passport which he was (the very last detail of which I can only suspect) and died doing this, I can only imagine...

A wasteless text might exist.

A wasteless text might exist.

I could protect this mind, and stay alive, but still be stuck.

So I began rereading old books I had already read. Once again.

In uniform, her language had no more illusion for her, you see.

And I would go down to a place called the Ohio bar and order, like, something totally not me, an egg cream.

And I would take a quiz and be reminded of driving.

Though it's possible for anti-illusion to maintain dance and costume.

It must actually.

And then I would have no need for continual absorption as I had in the days preceding.

That's how the property records are double-checked, are checked off.

She gets up on the nightstand.

That's when the sound is turned off.

She unscrews the vent.

That's how when she touches her at the mouth and then transcribes.

You— All of this— All of this... Is— (muffled speech) to...

YOU CROSS TO ME NOW SO SWEETLY
YOU MUST BE THE GREATEST GOOD I'VE SEEN
I THANK THE MOTHER
OF THIS EARTH FOR SUCH A BRILLIANT MOSS, YOUR GLANDS, AND
EXUBERANCE, YOU ARE MY MOTHER EARTH
I WANT TO SING YOUR NAME TO THE DEPTHS OF LONELINESS
COMMUNITY IS WHAT I'VE FOUND IN THOSE
WOODS AND NEED I SAY IT YOU HAD A WAY OF MAGIC
YOU HAD A WAY OF UNLEASHING ME FROM A THOUSAND PRISONS
YOU HAD A WAY OF SWEET, SWEET MAGIC!

the insides of this book

Test 11–19

Test 21–29

~~outside voices, please~~ 31–109

acknowledgments

The Adroit Journal, Berkeley Poetry Review, Chicago Review, Cloud Rodeo, Cosmonauts Avenue, Leveler, The Nation, Prelude, The Rumpus, So & So Magazine, word for/word, my sincere thanks to the editors of these journals for publishing some of the pieces from this book in their earlier forms and to their readers. Thank you as well to Dani Leder and Downs & Ross for commissioning page 93.

Valerie Hsiung is the author of *hummingbird et partygirl* (Essay Press),
Name Date of Birth Emergency Contact (The Gleaners),
YOU & ME FOREVER (Action Books), and *e f g* (Action Books).

RECENT CLEVELAND STATE UNIVERSITY POETRY CENTER PUBLICATIONS

Edited by Caryl Pagel & Hilary Plum

POETRY

World'd Too Much: The Selected Poetry of Russell Atkins
ed. Kevin Prufer and Robert E. McDonough
Advantages of Being Evergreen by Oliver Baez Bendorf
Dream Boat by Shelley Feller
My Fault by Leora Fridman
Orient by Nicholas Gulig
Twice There Was A Country by Alen Hamza
Age of Glass by Anna Maria Hong
In One Form to Find Another by Jane Lewty
50 Water Dreams by Siwar Masannat
daughterrarium by Sheila McMullin
The Bees Make Money in the Lion by Lo Kwa Mei-en
Residuum by Martin Rock
Festival by Broc Rossell
Sun Cycle by Anne Lesley Selcer
Bottle the Bottles the Bottles the Bottles by Lee Upton

ESSAYS

I Liked You Better Before I Knew You So Well by James Allen Hall
A Bestiary by Lily Hoang
Codependence by Amy Long
The Leftovers by Shaelyn Smith

TRANSLATIONS

Scorpionic Sun by Mohammed Khaïr-Eddine, translated by Conor Bracken
I Burned at the Feast: Selected Poems of Arseny Tarkovsky translated by
Philip Metres and Dimitri Psurtsev

For a complete list of titles visit www.csupoetrycenter.com